Reading
Together
Parents'
Handbook

Sue Ellis   Myra Barrs

WALKER BOOKS

AND SUBSIDIARIES

LONDON · BOSTON · SYDNEY · AUCKLAND

The Reading Together Series

As a parent, you play a very important part in helping your child to read. Encouraging children to develop a love of books and an interest in written language helps their literacy now and makes a difference to their whole future.

In this book we draw together tried and tested ways for you to help your child become confident with books and reading. We describe how children learn to read and include suggestions about writing and spelling too, answering many of the questions parents ask about their children's literacy.

This handbook will also help you to use the
Reading Together series, which it accompanies.
Using the *Reading Together* series makes it possible
for you to introduce your child to a variety of
carefully chosen stories, rhymes and information books.
As you do so, they will develop their own favourites
and begin to talk about them with real enthusiasm
and understanding.

We hope that *Reading Together* will provide you and your
child with much to enjoy now and for years to come.

Myra Barrs   Sue Ellis.

The Centre for Language in Primary Education

Learning at home

You probably don't remember just how you learned to read and write yourself, but you may be finding out more about how it works now, from watching your own children. Children pick up a lot about reading and writing by themselves, but they also need help in putting together all this information.

Babies and books

Even small babies find pleasure in language. They enjoy being sung to and read to, and they like it when you tell them stories and rhymes. All this is a good basis for their later enjoyment of books.

Reading aloud

From the beginning, making time to read with children is the key to making books come alive for them. Reading aloud is one of the main ways in which you help your children to become readers. And if you are a reader, the chances are that they will be too.

Joining in

All young children observe what adults do, and learn by imitation. They see us reading the newspaper or writing a shopping list and they want to join in.

Surrounded by words

Out and about, in the street, on buses, in supermarkets and public places, children are surrounded by written signs. Soon they want to know what these "say". You can help them by pointing out words and making it into a game.

Television

Children pick up all sorts of information about reading from television. They may recognize the titles of popular programmes, or brand names of the products in TV adverts. It's often one of the ways they learn their letters.

Starting to read

When they begin to learn to read, either at home or at school, children draw on all the different kinds of information they have gathered about books and reading. As well as learning letters, children need to realize above all that the point of reading is to get at what the book means.

Starting school

Schools try to build on the experiences of literacy that children bring with them from home. They aim not only to teach children to read the words on the page, but also to help them become readers who choose to read on their own. Children will stand a better chance of doing well in their schooling if they already enjoy reading and being read to, and are used to talking about books.

Reading aloud

Reading aloud is one of the most important ways you can help your child learn to read and write – and it's never too early to start! Through sharing books with parents, children learn to turn the pages, to talk about the story and the pictures, to join in with parts they know well, and gradually to recognize words on the page. All this helps to build their confidence and interest, and plays an important part in their development as successful readers.

Sharing books

Try to share books together every day: at bedtime, in the afternoon, while waiting at the doctor's surgery or sitting on the bus. Settling down to look at a book together can be a relaxing and rewarding experience for both parent and child in an often hectic day.

Different books

By reading aloud to your children, you can introduce them to different kinds of books and to the different worlds each book opens up. Variety is important, and in the *Reading Together* series children can experience a range of books: traditional and modern stories, rhymes, poetry, songs and information books.

Learning the "tunes"

Through reading aloud, children also become familiar with the individual rhythms and "tunes" of each story and learn to tell stories in their own way. They enjoy hearing the predictable rhythm of a nursery rhyme and the different voices in a story. Sometimes they will join in by humming along, by finishing a rhyme or by echoing what you've said. These experiences are a great help when children come to read the words themselves. Encourage your child to choose books for you to read to them. They might have a favourite they want to hear every night for a week or even longer!

Understanding the meanings

Reading aloud to children helps them understand how books work. They learn about the meanings in a story, the messages and the jokes, and they learn to predict what will happen next. Children begin to make connections between what happens in the book and their own lives.

Joining in

As children get to know a book they will begin to remember the story and join in as you read, especially with repeated phrases. They may enjoy the satisfaction of guessing the rhyme in a poem or finishing a well-known phrase in a story, so it's helpful to leave space for them to do so. The books in the *Reading Together* series encourage children to join in, making it easy for them to play a big part in reading with you.

Talking about books

Talking about the story and pictures adds to children's enjoyment and understanding. If your child asks questions or interrupts the reading by pointing to words they know or talking about the pictures, it's a good sign that they're interested and want to find out more. You can help them to talk about the book by saying things like, "I wonder why that happened?" or, "Can you guess what's going to happen next?" or, "Why do you like this book so much?" Children will often be reminded of their own experience by the books you read together and one story can spark many others! Talking about books is one of the best ways for children to get involved in stories and to feel like readers.

Talking about the pictures

The pictures help to tell the story and, in some books, tell more of the story than the words alone. Young children often talk their way through the book using the pictures to guide them. They might use their own words or remember the story by heart. This is not "cheating" but part of beginning to read. As children get older, the pictures continue to help them make good guesses about words they don't know.

Talking about the words

Another way young children will join in is by using knowledge of words they already know, like their name, to spot familiar letters and words in the books they share with you. You can respond to this interest by helping them to see the connections between, and patterns in, words, e.g.

Parent: "What does 'Spotty' sound like?"
Child: "Potty!"

Re-reading

Children get a lot of confidence and pleasure from books they know well, and re-reading helps them to see how books and stories work. It's important to keep re-reading old favourites. When children begin learning to read, their knowledge of a familiar book will help them as they start to notice more about the words on the page. You can encourage them to look more carefully at the words and letters in books they know well.

Revisiting books

Even when children begin to read for themselves, they may still want to re-read familiar books quite frequently. This doesn't mean that they are standing still in their reading: progress is not always a matter of going on to the next book. Even experienced readers enjoy re-reading. Tapes of favourite stories provide another way for children to hear stories again and can help them with matching the words they hear to the words on the page.

Retelling

By hearing a book again and again, young children often get to know a story so well that they can retell it in their own words. Re-reading makes retelling possible and this is a valuable way for children to learn how the story goes. You can encourage your child to use the book cover or the pictures to help with the retelling.

Acting out the story

Children may also enjoy acting out a story, sometimes using the language of the book. This gives them a chance to try out what they've learned and make it their own; they are learning how to be a storyteller, and how to make up dialogue. You can encourage this kind of play by providing them with a few dressing-up clothes and home-made props. Stories like *Walking through the Jungle*, and songs such as *The Wheels on the Bus*, are fun to perform together. You can act them out at home, or even when you're walking along! Children also like to act out stories with toy animals or small figures. They may draw a picture of a story and talk their way through it, or they might change stories by making up their own versions. All these kinds of acting-out play can be a basis for their later story writing.

Beginning to read

Between four and seven, most children begin to read for themselves. They do this in very different ways. At first, some may "read" the book by remembering the story and making up their own words. Others may want to get every word right, and be unwilling to guess at all. Some keep going at all costs; others read hesitantly. It is important to respond to children as individuals. Gradually let them take over as much of the reading as they can. They may need to be helped to look more carefully at the actual words, or they may have to be encouraged to move the story along and worry less about mistakes.

Words, letters and sounds

As children begin to look more closely at the print on the page, you can help them by pointing out words they know. These could be names, or words they know from other contexts (such as "baby" or "exit"). When they recognize particular words or letters, you can help them find places where these recur ("Let's find another place where it says 'bus' ").

You can pick up on this interest in letters by helping them to make links between words that look or sound alike (e.g. words that rhyme). It's useful to have a set of alphabet bricks or tiles, to look at alphabet books – or make your own. You can play letter games together, making lists of names, or building collections of words they know that begin with the same letter.

Games like this can be the best way for children to learn about print. But it will be important not to spoil the reading of stories by focusing too closely on the letters. It can be better to satisfy children's growing interest in written language by helping them to write.

Encouraging independence
If children get stuck when they are reading, encourage them to have a go and use everything they know – the information in the pictures, their memory of the story, and their knowledge of letters and sounds – to make sense of the book. The trick is in sensing when to give them information and how much to provide. A good rule is to back off if a child seems to be getting anxious, or reluctant to read.

Beginning to write

Children learn a lot about reading from their own attempts at writing. When they write, they have to think carefully about how words sound and how they look. You can encourage children to write from very early on, by helping them to put their name in birthday cards or by sending their drawings and messages to relatives and friends.

Wanting to write

Young children are often eager to write. They might begin by drawing pictures, and then want to write their own name or a story to go with the pictures. This writing may not be easy for you to read, but your child will know what it says. You can build on this interest by helping them to make lists of names or encouraging them to write their stories using the letters and words they know.

Watching you write

Children can also write by dictating to you. Get them to tell you a story and write it down for them. They learn a lot by watching you write, by seeing how you make the letters, and by telling you how they think some of the words begin. Afterwards, you can read the story back to them, or they can read it for themselves. Later they may want to write down stories they know well. You could help them to make their own little books, perhaps taking it in turns to write the story down.

Signs and labels

As they grow more independent, you can also encourage children to make labels and notices. They may enjoy making their own signs – for the different rooms in the house, for coat pegs, for the door of the fridge, or for their toybox. Show them how to form the letters clearly so people can read them.

Spelling

As children grow more confident about writing, encourage them to write as much as they can on their own, but also be prepared to supply spellings sometimes and to show them how something looks in grown-up writing. At school they will be encouraged to have a go at spelling on their own, but they will also need to realize quite early on that not all words in English are spelled like they sound.

Home and school

When children go to school, they build on the knowledge they've picked up at home, including valuable experiences of stories and books. They will continue to need just as much help and encouragement with their reading at home as before.

Reading at home
It is important not to change the way you read with children, or read to them less frequently, just because they are now learning to read at school. They still need lots of experiences of books, stories and being read to. Don't feel that reading needs to become a more formal or serious business at this stage, with most of the emphasis on the words. The story, the meanings, the pictures and the words are all important.

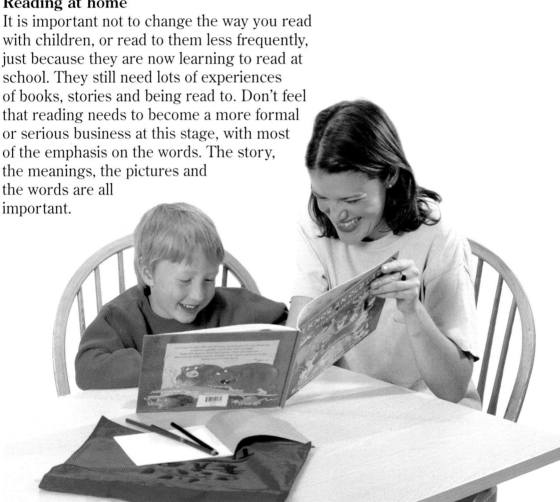

Starting school

When children join a school or nursery there is usually a meeting between parents and teachers for the school to find out about your child. They are interested to know about the books your child enjoys, about favourite rhymes and stories, knowledge of the alphabet, and whether your child likes to write.

School approach

Many schools recognize the important part parents play in children's reading development and send home books regularly for children to share with their families. Sometimes parents are invited to help their child choose books from school at the beginning or end of the day. There may be "home-school notebooks" sent home with children's reading books for parents and teachers to write down comments about a child's reading, choice of books and progress. This is a valuable way for parents and teachers to exchange information and work together to support children as readers.

Parents in school

Many schools welcome parents into the classroom to read to children and share books with them. If you can be involved, it is a good way to learn about your child's experience at school and give valuable support to them and other children.

Reading in more than one language

Some children are fortunate in being able to speak in more than one language. Whenever possible, it is important that they should be helped to read in the languages they know.

Choosing books

Choosing books for your children can be a great pleasure, but it can be daunting too. In libraries, bookshops and supermarkets there is so much choice, it can be hard to know where to start looking. The *Reading Together* series makes the task easier by offering a range of books which provides lots of support to children reading them.

How do we choose?

It's always helpful to think about how we, as adults, choose a book to read or a film to see. We might make a choice because of a recommendation by someone we trust or we'll read another book by an author whose books we've read before. Sometimes we'll browse along the bookshelves and pick up a book because it looks new or interesting or because it's been on TV. These are all useful ways of choosing books for your child.

Children are individuals

From the moment a child is born, parents are aware of their child's particular way of doing things and, over time, will discover what interests them and how they learn best. Choosing books that appeal to your child's passion for animals, tractors or dinosaurs, their love of songs, jokes or fairytales, is a good start.

Trust your own response

You will probably share a book with your child many many times, so it's a good idea to consider carefully whether you think they will like it – and whether you do! Ask yourself if it's the kind of book your child could go back to and enjoy more and more each time. Children can have even more variety if more than one person in the family does the choosing.

Who's reading?

Sometimes you will want to read books to your children that they are ready to listen to but that are too difficult for them to read for themselves. Then there are books where children can share the reading, joining in with familiar rhymes and phrases. And there are books which children feel confident to read or tell to you. When choosing books for your child, think about which of you would be doing the reading.

Sources of books

- Many *schools* encourage children to choose books from the classroom or school library to read at home.
- Visiting the *local library* helps to widen the range of books your child can get to know even further and means you can try out a new book and take it back if it's too difficult or not quite as interesting as you'd hoped.
- It's also important for children to own some of their own books and to have favourites that they can return to like old friends. *Bookshops and supermarkets* have a wide choice of books and children can begin choosing from a very young age, with your guidance.
- *Bookclubs* have a range of books to choose from by mail order and can be a useful source of information about new books.

Parents' questions

I feel I don't know enough about how to read aloud to my two year old. I even feel a bit silly doing it.

You already talk to your child and your voice is one of the sounds they most enjoy. Read the story to yourself first, so you get to know it, and then just have a go – you'll get better as you go along. You could pick up some tips from listening to story tapes.

At what stage should I teach him the sounds and letters? Does he need to know the alphabet? Should he learn it with capitals or small letters?

You will find that at about three years old children can begin to take a real interest in the alphabet, and especially in letters that mean something to them – like the letters in their name. You can foster this interest by having alphabets (books, friezes or posters, alphabet bricks, plastic letters on the fridge) around the home. You may enjoy looking for letters your child knows (both capitals and small letters are important) when you go out shopping. Children can begin to associate sounds with letters through making collections of words they know around particular letters – you can make these into posters or little books.

My five year old will "read" the book she brings home from school to me, but she's not really reading it, she's just remembering it. I'm worried – if she really thinks it's all right to make up the words, how will she ever learn that there is a right way to do it?

Remembering the words is one of the ways children learn about stories and how it feels to be a reader. As their confidence grows, they will start to pay more attention to the words on the page, recognizing familiar words and noticing similarities between words. You can help by asking them to look for words or letters they know and drawing their attention to particular words they have seen elsewhere. Retelling the story for you to write it down will help them to notice more about the way the words look and how they are built up. If children are still relying mainly on their memory of the story by the time they're about six, then they will need more help and more practice with writing and with looking carefully at the print. Help them by making alphabets and teaching them ways of focusing on the print, such as pointing to the words as they read.

My child reads happily when he's playing with his computer and he reads comics, but he doesn't enjoy the books he has to bring home from school. Should I talk to the teacher?

Your son is like a number of other children, many of them boys, who enjoy certain kinds of reading much more than others. They may like information books, or books with a lot of pictures and graphics – and these are not always the kinds of books that are available in schools' reading programmes. By all means tell the teacher what you've noticed about your son's reading. It could be important information which would help her in planning for his progress. You could also begin to look for books which share features with the kind of reading he likes – picture books with cartoon-style illustrations or highly illustrated information books, for example – so that he can begin to widen his range as a reader.

How do you help a reluctant reader? I want to help give back the pleasure to my son who's beginning to find reading is just a task.

Your son may have been feeling that reading is just about getting the words right. There are a lot of children who learn to read but who don't choose to read. It's important to take the pressure off and show that reading can be fun. You can easily do this by sharing books with your son and reading to him, as well as expecting him to read to you. Many parents stop reading to their children as soon as they can read for themselves, but it is really important to go on reading aloud to children and exploring new books – even when they're eight, nine or ten. Take time to talk about the books together and go back to favourites. Your son may also need some help with choosing new books if he's bored with his current reading.

I'd like to know what's going on when my child stops and thinks what the word is. How does he decide?

When children are learning to read they are juggling many different kinds of knowledge and information to help them read the words on the page. They are using their knowledge of their spoken language, or languages, of story and print. When they meet a word they don't know in a story, they will predict the word by asking themselves: "What could it be?", "What makes sense here?" or "What sounds right?" and by using the letters and groups of letters they know to help them check their guess. The pictures provide useful clues, and rhymes help children to pick up more clues from the text. If children are only shown one way to guess a word, it makes it harder for them to be a fluent reader. To be successful readers they need to use a variety of strategies, drawing on all the clues in the text and illustrations.

I've heard it helps children's reading to teach them songs and rhymes. How does this work?

Many reading experts now think that children learn a lot about the features of language from songs and rhymes. These strongly patterned texts may help to make children more aware of the sounds of language. Rhyme is particularly helpful in drawing attention to the endings of words, and to similarities between words. Children who have plenty of experience of songs and nursery rhymes seem to find learning to read more straightforward; they are quick to focus on the links between letters and sounds, and they can see the patterns in the words they know. So as well as enjoying singing songs and reading nursery rhymes and poems with your child, you can also feel confident that this kind of pleasurable activity is very much part of learning to read.

How can I help my child when she makes mistakes?

To read confidently and fluently, children need to take risks and make mistakes and they need the space to do this. They learn by noticing and correcting their own errors, and this takes time. Children's confidence in themselves as readers can be undermined if adults jump in each time the child stumbles over a word. It's often more helpful to give occasional prompts, or a word, in order to keep the story flowing.

When my six year old picks up a new book to read to us she really struggles, yet she's a good reader. Why?

It's always hard for any reader, adult or child, to read aloud "cold" without knowing the tune and rhythm of a text. It would help enormously if you read all or part of it aloud first to give her an idea of how the story goes. Make the first reading of the book a pleasurable opportunity to get to know it and to spend time talking about parts that your child finds interesting.

My four year old asks me to write things down for her and really doesn't want to have a go at writing herself. But she's into copying, and copies my writing. Should I push her to write more for herself?

All children learn by imitation and your four year old is certainly learning even if she isn't attempting to write by herself yet. She is obviously interested in writing and wants very much to see how it's done. Perhaps she is not the kind of learner who likes to take too many risks with a new piece of learning. You will have to take your cue from her, but you are already helping her a lot by writing down what she wants to say and showing it to her.

Our local school lets children spell everything in their own way, and I cannot see how they will ever learn to spell correctly if this goes on.

Much more is expected of young children learning to write now; instead of just copying under adults' writing they are encouraged to write independently from the start. To do this they have to use what they have got and (usually) spell the words in the way that they sound. In this way they do develop a strong sense of the relationships between letters and sounds, so it helps their reading. It also means that they can write much more than if they had to ask for every word. Of course, you are right that this kind of invented spelling cannot go on for ever and certainly by the end of the second year in school children should have been shown that they cannot rely only on the sound of words as a guide to their spelling. Good spellers need to attend closely to the look of words and notice how they are constructed.

Other children are doing better than my child. What can I do?

First of all, learning to read is not a race, and you must be careful not to get too competitive on your child's behalf. Remember how different children are in learning to talk and learning to walk; learning to read is a bit like that. Children will vary in how rapidly they take on reading, and worrying about this is not likely to help them. In fact, if you are communicating your anxiety to your child, you may be making him anxious too, and this will not improve the situation. All that being said, if you still feel that your child is progressing much too slowly compared with his age group, then you do need to signal this quite strongly to the teacher and hear what she advises. You can help by ensuring that you read with your child every day, encouraging him to join in as much as he can. He may simply need a lot more experience of reading.

Is it going to be confusing for my children, or hold them back, if they learn to read in their first language as well as in English?

Learning to talk, to read and write in more than one language is a real asset and needs to be encouraged. Having access to more than one language helps children to understand more clearly how languages work and to use them more flexibly. Often, children who are fully fluent bilinguals are more successful as readers.

The authors and publisher would like to thank the following
for appearing in the photographs in this book:

Jonathan Birkett Julian Birkett Lily Birkett Clare Boucher Maxine Edney
Jack Haggard Alice Hall Cerise Hall Marcus Harris Simone Harris Daniel Huynh
James Howell Catherine Jessop Isabel Jessop Lorraine Kenton Myron Kenton-Dawes
Anna Lilly Jack Lilly Matthew Lilly Thomas Lilly Laura Main Ellen
Finn Nightingale Michelle Nightingale Zoë Philby Eve Stotesbury
Grace Stotesbury Nick Turpin

Thanks also to the following for their help
with the parents' questions:

Sally Brightling
Chrissie Gray
Susan Silverstein
Richard Stotesbury

First published 1998 by Walker Books Ltd
87 Vauxhall Walk, London SE11 5HJ

This edition published 2005

2 4 6 8 10 9 7 5 3

Text © 1998 CLPE
Photographs © 1998 Paul Forrester

Printed in China

British Library Cataloguing in Publication Data:
a catalogue record for this book
is available from the British Library

ISBN 1-4063-0065-9

www.walkerbooks.co.uk